HINDI

MADE EASY

BOOK I

(सरल हिन्दी)

प्रथम भाग

FOR BEGINNERS

By
J.S. Nagra M.A., M.Ed., Ph.D.
AND
S.K. Nagra B.A. B.Ed.

Published by :
Nagra Publications
399, Ansty Road, Coventry, U.K., CV2 3BQ.
Tel & Fax 02476 617314

ISBN 1 870383 03 6

1st Edition : November 1984
2nd Revised Edition : July 1988
Reprinted : June 1992, October 2000, May 2006

1. D.T.F. Asian Bookshop, 117, Soho Road, Handsworth, Birmingham B21 9ST. Tel : 0121 515 1183.
2. Independent Publishing Co. Ltd., 38, Kennington Lane, London SE 114 LS. Tel : 0207 735 2101.
3. Indian Bookshop, 55 Warren Street, London W1T 5NW. Tel : 0207 380 0622.
4. Gardners Books Ltd., 1 Whittle Drive, Eastbourne, East Sussex, BN23 6QH. Tel : 01323 521555.

Acknowledgements

Our sincere thanks are due to Dr. Mangat Rai Bhardwaj who read the first draft of the book and gave valuable suggestions.

Our thanks are due to Mr. Yash Pal Rai Sharma M.A., M.Ed. and Mr. Vidya Sagar Sharma M.A. for their suggestions.

We are grateful to Mr. Raghbir Akant (graphic designer) for illustrating and designing the book.

J.S. Nagra
S.K. Nagra
(Authors)

Introduction

This book is the first one in the 'Hindi Made Easy' series. It is meant primarily for beginners of Hindi. It may be of use to more advanced learners and teachers of students whose first or dominant language is English.

Slightly modified Roman script is used throughout to facilitate the learning of Hindi sounds, but not to replace the Hindi script. I believe that learning the Hindi script is an exciting intellectual adventure which must not be missed by anyone interested in the language, though it is perfectly possible to learn spoken Hindi without learning the Hindi script.

All learners are advised to listen attentively to native speakers of Hindi. The Hindi script represents the Hindi sounds fairly systematically (sometimes more so than the Roman alphabet represents the English sounds), but no script is perfect.

The meanings of some of the words used in each lesson are given in the lesson itself. For the meanings of the other words, consult the list on pages 51 to 60.

J.S. Nagra
S.K. Nagra

Notes on Pronunciation

VOWLES (स्वर)

Hindi has ten vowel sounds

अ	a	as in	the	English	word	about
आ	ā	,,	,,	,,	,,	arm
इ	i	,,	,,	,,	,,	sit
ई	ī	,,	,,	,,	,,	seat
उ	u	,,	,,	,,	,,	put
ऊ	ū	,,	,,	,,	,,	boot

ए e
ओ o } No exact equivalent in English, ए can be heard in words like 'May' 'gate' etc. in the speech of the Indian speakers of English. Similarly, ओ is found in their speech in words like 'go' 'pole' etc.

ऐ ai
औ au } Many speakers of Hindi pronounce each as a compound vowel, gliding from short 'a' to short 'i' or to short 'u'. You can pronounce them as they do. But we recommend that ऐ be pronounced like the vowel in the English word 'cat' but it should be made slightly longer. Similarly, औ can be pronounced like the vowel in 'pot' but made slightly longer.

Consonants

Since we had to follow the principle of one sound, one symbol and since there are more sounds in Hindi than there are letters in the English alphabet we had to add bars and dots to some of the English letters.

A bar over the symbols (as in ā, ī, ū) shows that the sound is long.

A dot under a symbol (as in ṭ, ḍ, ṇ, ṛ) shows that the sound is produced by curling the tongue against the roof of the mouth. It is very important to produce these sounds in this way and not in the English way otherwise there can be confusion. Without dots, t, d, n should be pronounced as in French and not as in English. (look at diagrams on page 7 very carefully).

When h occurs after k, t, ṭ ,c, p (as in kh th ṭh ch chh ph) it should not be pronounced as a separate sound but the sound preceding h should be pronounced with a strong puff of air.

The symbol ~ when placed over vowel letters indicates that the vowel is pronounced both through the nose and the mouth.

Pronunciation of Hindi

ṭ, ṭh, ḍ, ḍh, ṇ, ṛ, ṛh
and
t, th, d, dh

Look at the following diagrams carefully and note the position of the tongue for pronunciation of the Hindi sounds compared with that for the English sounds. If you want your spoken Hindi to be properly understood, avoid pronouncing these sounds like the English t and d.

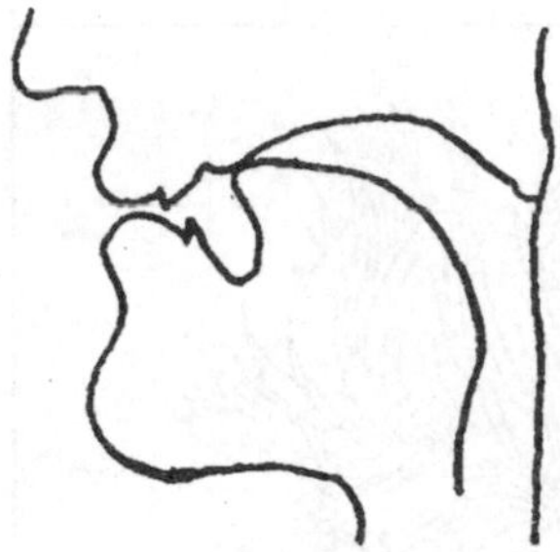

When you pronounce the English t and d, the tip and the upper side of your tongue touches the gumridge behind the upper teeth.

English t and d

It is important that when you pronounce the Hindi ṭ, ṭh, ḍ, ḍh, ṇ, ṛ and ṛh (ट, ठ, ड, ढ, ण, ड़, ढ़) you should curl your tongue backward and the lower side of your tongue touch the hard palate.

Hindi ṭ, ṭh, ḍ, ḍh, ṇ, ṛ, ṛh
ट ठ ड ढ ण ड़ ढ़

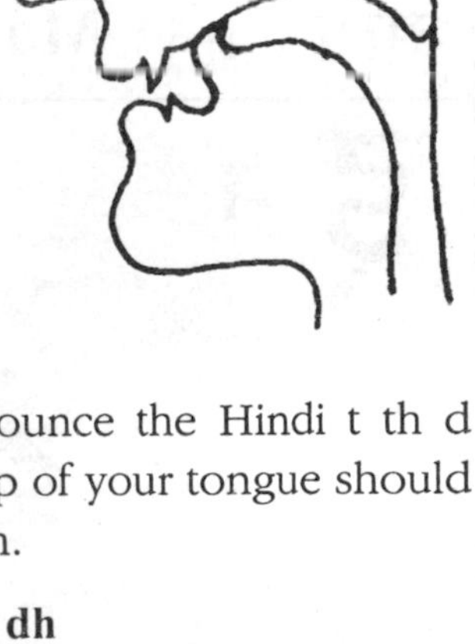

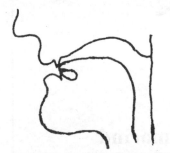

When you pronounce the Hindi t th d dh त थ द ध the tip of your tongue should touch your teeth.

Hindi t th d dh
त थ द ध

Pomegranate **अ** **-a**

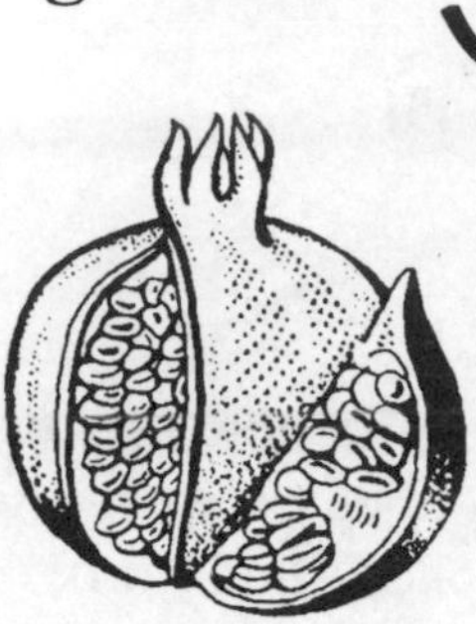

अनार (anār)

Guava

अमरूद (amrūd)

आ **-ā**

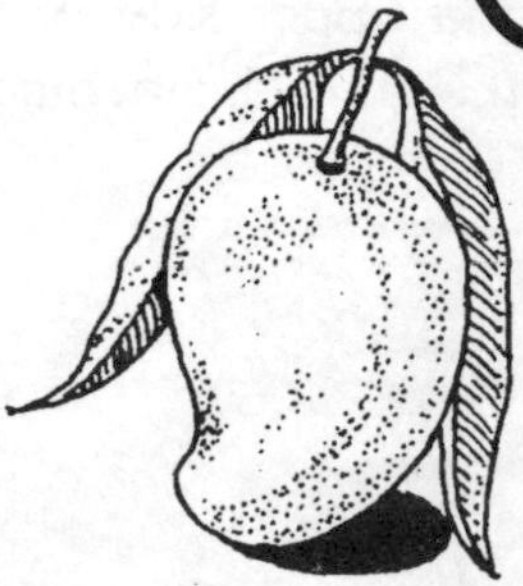

आम (ām) **Mango**

आग (āg) **Fire**

इ **-i**

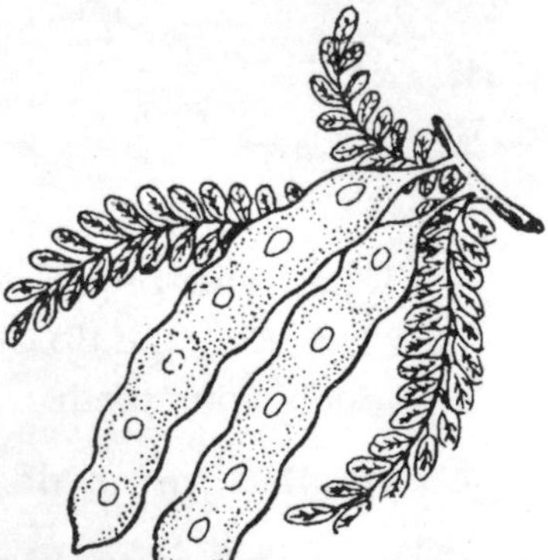

इमली (imlī) **Tamarind**

ई -ī

ईख (īkh) **Sugarcane**

उ -u

उल्लू (ullū) **Owl**

ऊ -ū

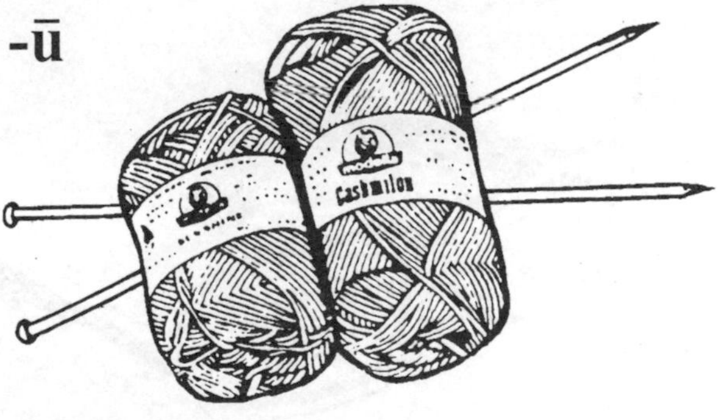

ऊन (ūn) **Wool**

ऋ -ri

ऋषि (rishi) **Hermit**

ए -e

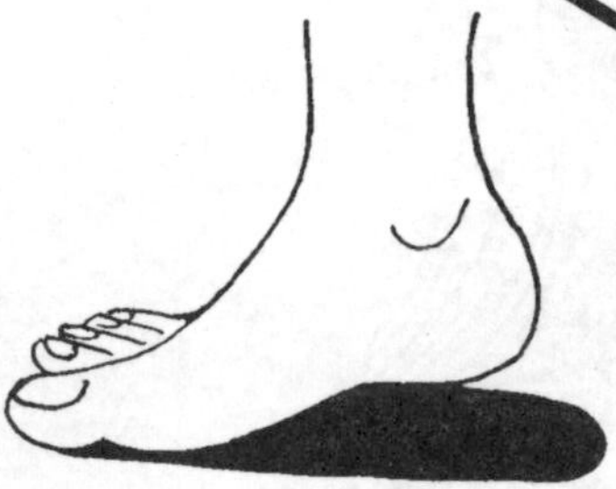

एड़ी (eṛī) **Heel**

एक (ek) **One**

ऐ -ai

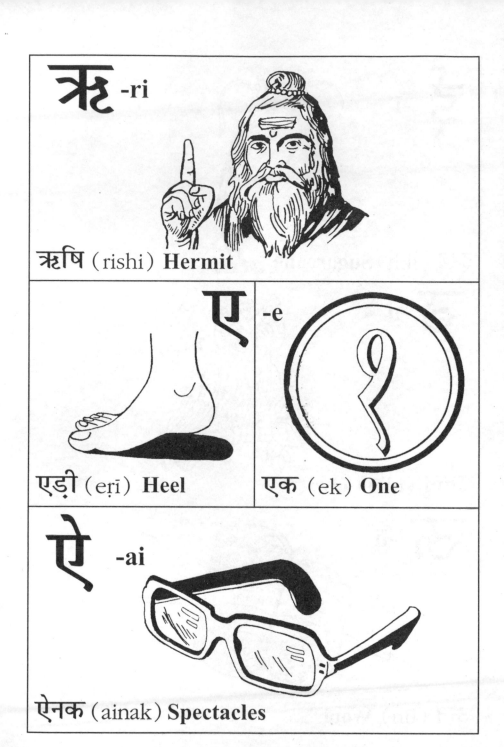

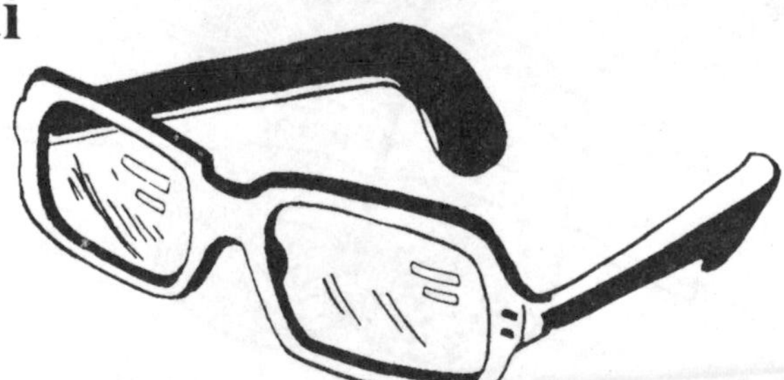

ऐनक (ainak) **Spectacles**

ओ **-o**

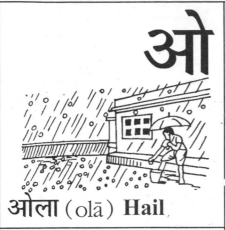

ओला (olā) **Hail**

ओढ़नी (Oṛhnī) **Shawl**

औ **-au**

औरत (aurat) **Woman**

Medicine

औषध (aushadh)

अं **-ang**

अंगूर (angūr) **Grapes**

अः **-ah** **Laugh**

अःहः (ah: h: h:)

Pigeon

क

-k

कबूतर (kabūtar)

कमल (kamal) **Lotus**

Rabbit

ख

-kh

Muskmelon

खरगोश (khargosh)

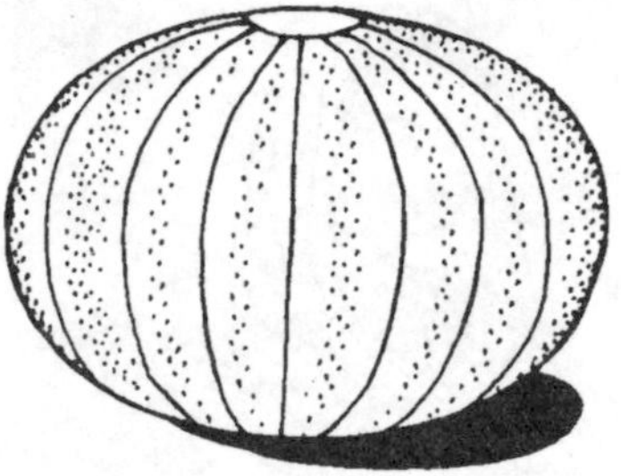

खरबूजा (kharbūjā)

ग

-g

गाय (gāy) **Cow**

गधा (gadhā) **Donkey**

घ -gha

घड़ी (ghaṛī) **Watch**

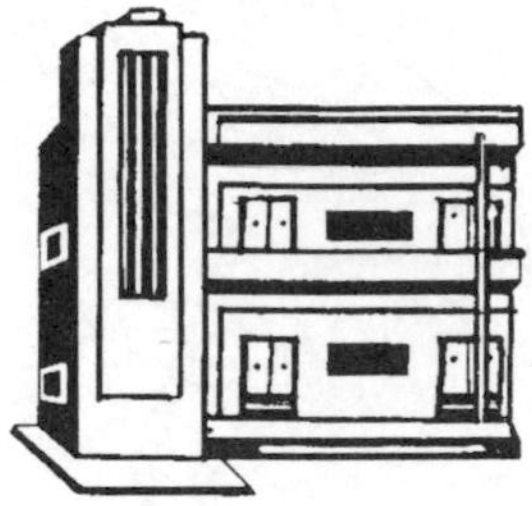

घर (ghar) **House**

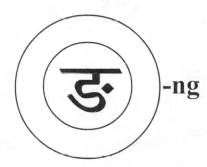

ङ -ng

This letter is not used to begin a word

च -ch

Spoon

चम्मच (chammach)

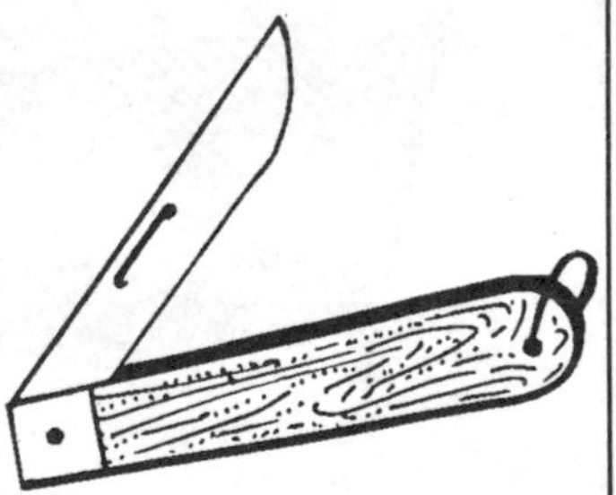

चाकू (chākū) **Knife**

Umbrella

छ -chh

छतरी (chhatarī)

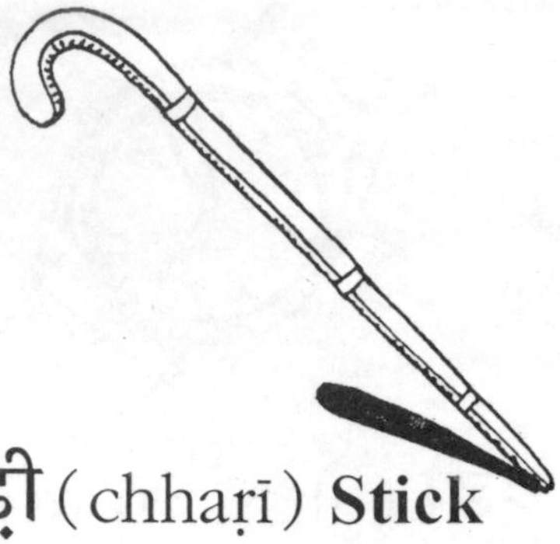

छड़ी (chhaṛī) **Stick**

ज -ja

जहाज़ (jahāz) **Ship**

जग (jag) **Jug**

झ -jh

झंडा (jhanḍā) **Flag**

झरना (jharnā) **Spring**

ङ -ng

This letter is not used to begin a word

ट -ṭ

टमाटर (ṭamāṭar) **Tomato**

Brazier

ठ -ṭh

ठठेरा (ṭhaṭherā)

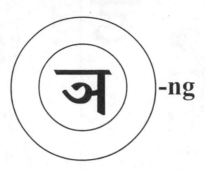

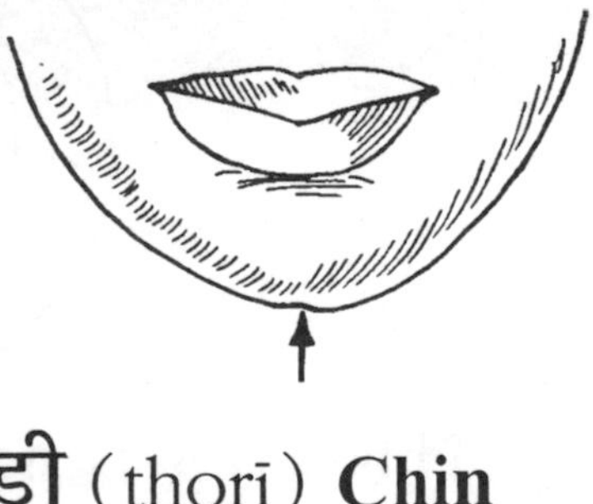

ठोड़ी (thoṛī) **Chin**

Postman ड

डाकिया (ḍākiyā)

-ḍ

डाकू (ḍākū) **Dacoit**

ढ

ढकना (ḍhaknā) **Lid**

-ḍh **Musical Instrument**

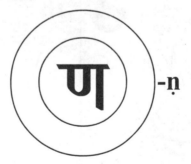

ढप (ḍhap)

ण -ṇ

This letter is not used to begin a word

त

तोता (totā) **Parrot**

-t **Balance**

तराज़ू (tarāzū)

थ

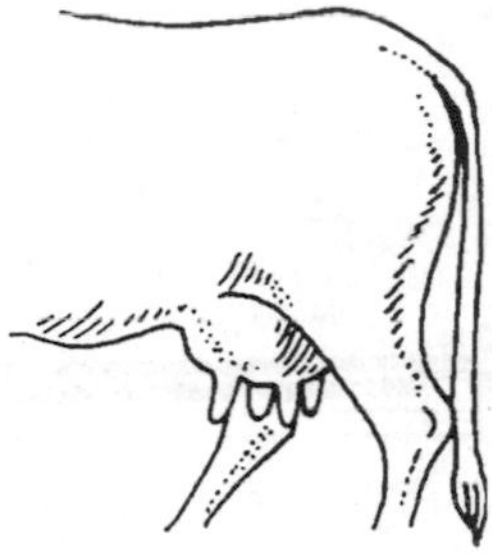

थन (than) **Nipple**

-th **Tharmos**

थरमस (tharmas)

द

दवात (dawāt) **Inkpot**

-d

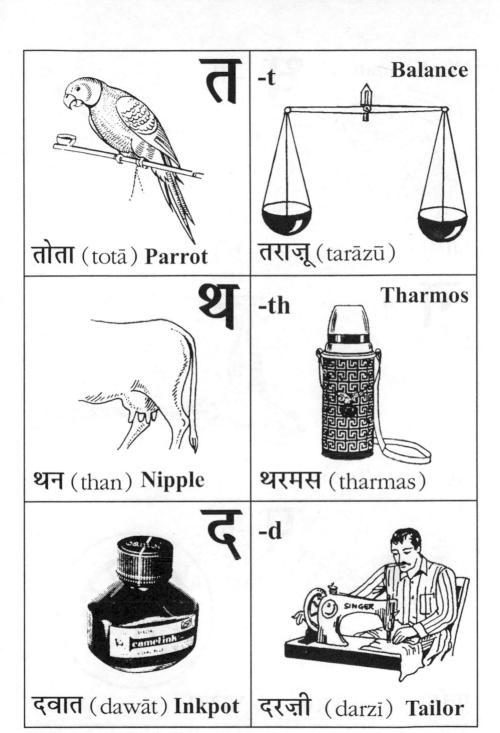

दरज़ी (darzī) **Tailor**

Washerman ध

धोबी (dhobī)

-dh

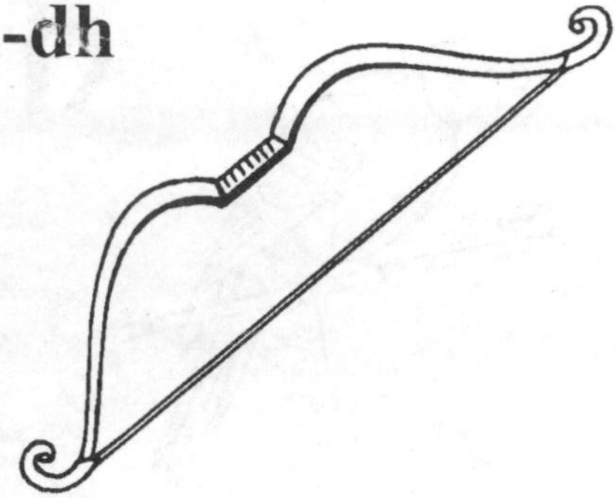

धनुष (dhanush) **Bow**

न -n

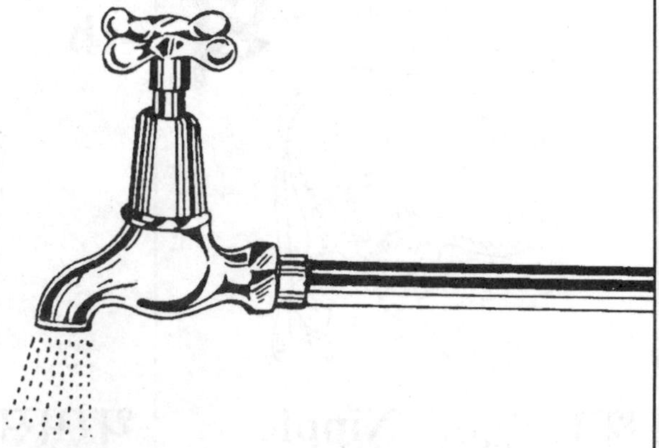

नल (nal) **Tap**

प -p

पतंग (patang) **Kite**

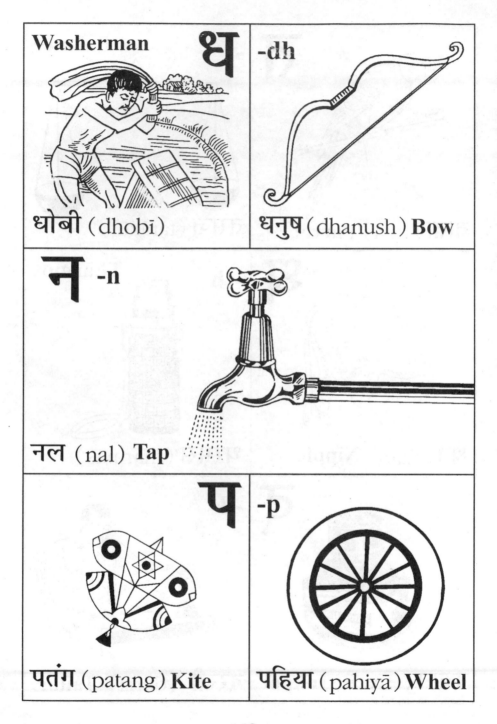

पहिया (pahiyā) **Wheel**

फ -ph

फल (phal) **Fruit**

फरसा (pharsā) **Axe**

ब -b

बकरी (bakrī) **Goat**

बछिया (bachhiyā) **Calf**

भ -bh

भेड़ (bheṛ) **Sheep**

म -m

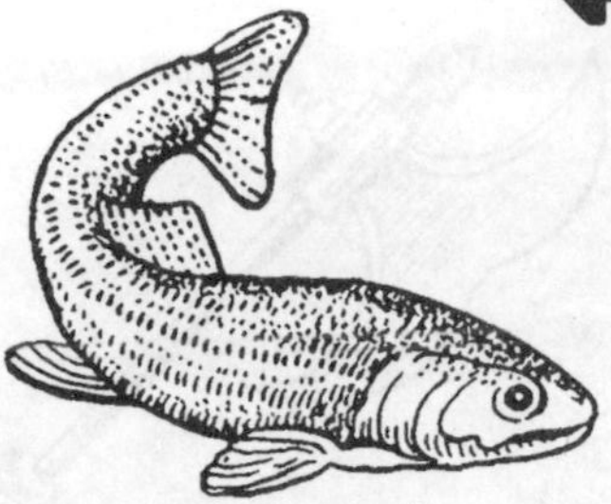

मछली (machhalī) **Fish**

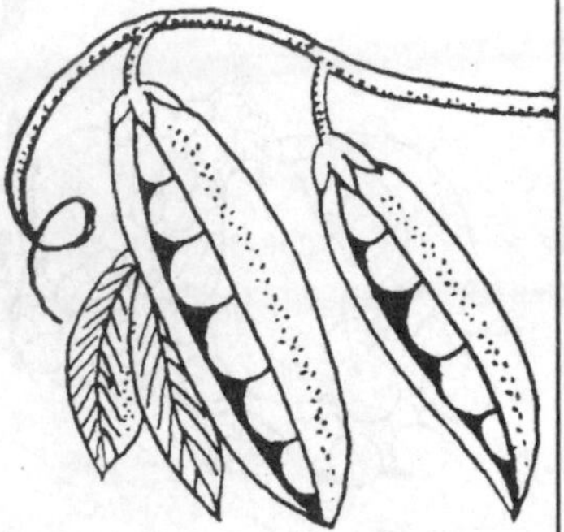

मटर (maṭar) **Pea**

Aeroplane

य -y

यान (हवा) (yān) (vāyu)

यक्का (yakkā) **Tonga**

र -r

रस्सी (rassī) **Rope**

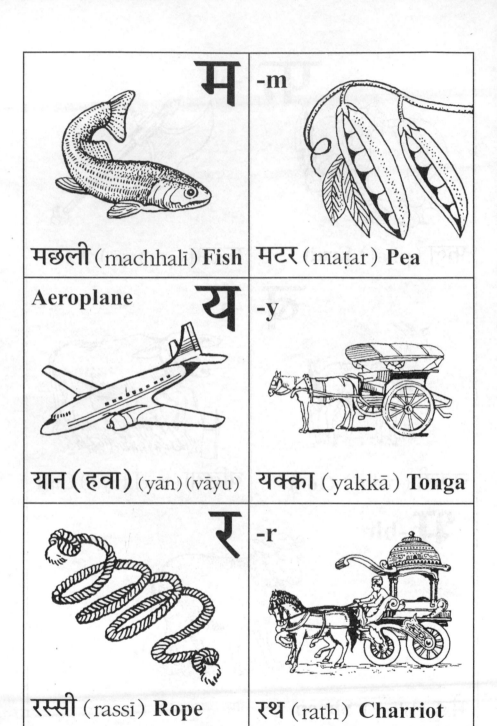

रथ (rath) **Charriot**

ल -l

लड़की (laṛakī) **Girl**

लट्टू (laṭṭū) **Top**

व -v

वर्षा (varshā) **Rain**

वन (van) **Forest**

श -sh

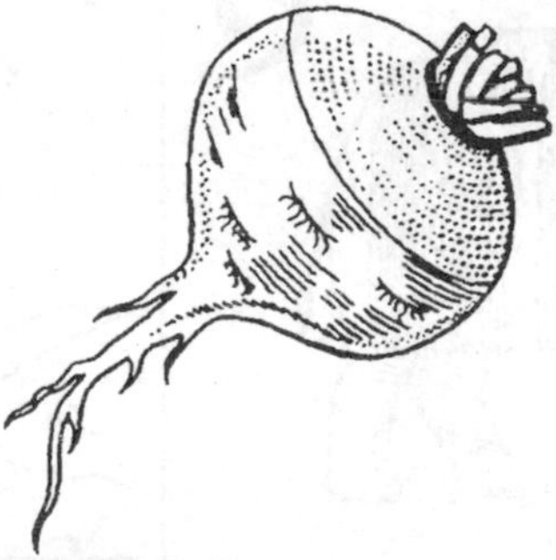

शलगम (shalgam) **Turnip**

ष -sh

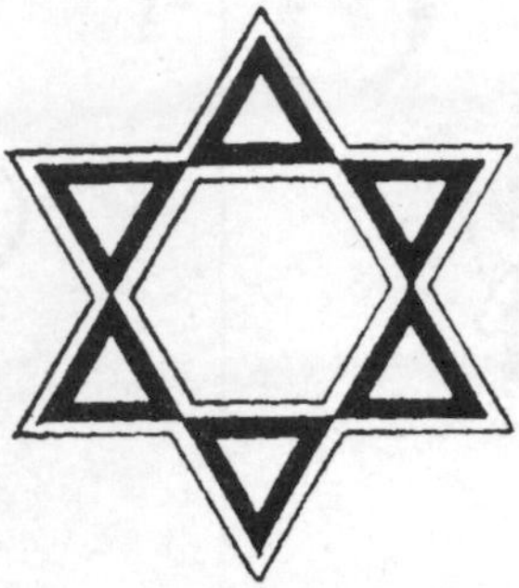

षट्कोण (shaṭkoṇ) **Hexagon**

स -s

साँप (sā̃p) **Snake**

ह -h

हाथी (hāthī) **Elephant**

हरिण (hariṇ) **Deer**

क्ष **-ksh**

क्षत्रिय (kshatriya) **Warrior**

त्र **-tr**

त्रिशूल (trishūl) **Trishul**

ज्ञ **-gya**

ज्ञानी (gyānī) **Scholar**

Hindi Alphabet

अ	आ	इ	ई	उ	ऊ	ऋ
a	ā	i	ī	u	ū	ri
ए	ऐ	ओ	औ	अं	अः	
e	ai	o	au	ang	ah	
क	ख	ग	घ	ङ		
k	kh	g	gh	ng		
च	छ	ज	झ	ञ		
ch	chh	j	jh	ng		
ट	ठ	ड	ढ	ण		
ṭ	ṭh	ḍ	ḍh	ṇ		
त	थ	द	ध	न		
t	th	d	dh	n		
प	फ	ब	भ	म		
p	ph	b	bh	m		
य	र	ल	व	श		
y	r	l	v	sh		
ष	स	ह	क्ष	त्र		
sh	s	h	ksh	tr		
ज्ञ	ड़	ढ़				
gy	ṛ	ṛh				

पहचान के लिए अक्षर
(Letters for Recognition)

र	ए	ऐ	स	ण	ख
व	ब	क	फ	प	ष
भ	झ	त्र	ग	न	त
म	ट	ढ	द	ठ	ङ
ड	उ	ऊ	अ	आ	ओ
औ	अं	अः	ऋ	य	थ
ल	ध	च	ज	ञ	इ
घ	ई	छ	ह	क्ष	श

Note : The learners should carefully note the construction of each letter with points dissimilarity. He should practice writing each letter a number of times independently.

There are however a few letters which give a different sound when a dot is put under them e.g.

ज़	**फ़**
z	**f**

How to Write Hindi

अ	आ	इ
ई	उ	ऊ
ऋ	ए	ऐ
ओ	औ	अं
	अः	

क	ख	ग	घ	ङ
च	छ	ज	झ	ञ
ट	ठ	ड	ढ	ण
त	थ	द	ध	न
प	फ	ब	भ	म
य	र	ल	व	श
ष	स	ह	क्ष	त्र

How to Write Hindi

अ आ इ

ई उ ऊ

ऋ ए ऐ

ओ औ अं

अः

How to Write Hindi

क	ख	ग	घ	ङ
च	छ	ज	झ	ञ
ट	ठ	ड	ढ	ण
त	थ	द	ध	न
प	फ	ब	भ	म
य	र	ल	व	श
ष	स	ह	क्ष	त्र
		ज्ञ		

Words made by combining two, three and four letters
दो, तीन तथा चार अक्षरों वाले शब्द

स् + अ = स

सच
(Sach) **Truth**

कह
(Kah) **Speak**

फल
(Phal) **Fruit**

बस
(Bas) **Bus**

जल
(Jal) **Water**

नल
(Nal) **Tap**

चख
(Chakh) **Taste**

पढ़
(Paṛh) **Read**

घर
(Ghar) **House**

नहर
(Nahar) **Canal**

च् + अ = च

टहल
(Ṭahal) **Walk**

सड़क
(Saṛak) **Road**

शहद
(Shahad) **Honey**

मदन
(Madan) **Boy's name**

कलम
(Kalam) **Pen**

कमल
(Kamal) **Lotus**

महल
(Mahal) **Palace**

बत्तख
(Batakh) **Duck**

कसरत
(Kasrat) **Exercise**

अजगर
(Ajgar) **Boa**

बरतन
(Bartan) **Vessel**

शरबत
(Sharbat) **Syrup**

दशरथ
(Dashrath) **An Indian King**

बरगद
(Bargad) **Banyan**

टमटम
(Ṭamṭam) **A carriage**

पनघट
(Panghaṭ) **Well**

नटखट
(Naṭkhaṭ) **Naughty**

सच कह। फल चख। बस पर चढ़। नल पर जल भर। उठ अब घर चल। नहर पर टहल। मदन शहद चख। मदन सड़क पर बच कर चल। कसरत कर। बरतन पनघट पर रख। टमटम पर चढ़ कर घर चल। नटखट न बन।

(Symbol ा) sounds as 'ā'

आ की मात्रा आ = ा

ख + आ = ा = खा   ल + आ = ा = ला

पाठ
(Pāṭh) **Lesson**

याद
(Yād) **Remember**

नाम
(Nām) **Name**

काम
(Kām) **Work**

हार
(Hār) **Necklace**

आम
(ām) **Mango**

राम
(Rām) **Ram**

डाल
(Ḍāl) **Branch**

चला
(Chalā) **To go**

सदा
(Sadā) **Always**

धान
(Dhān) **Paddy**

चार
(Chār) **Four**

साफ़
(Sāf) **Clean**

हाथ
(Hāth) **Hand**

नाथ
(Nāth) **Boy's name**

चाचा
(Chāchā) **Uncle**

छाता
(Chhātā) **Umbrella**

काला
(Kālā) **Black**

माला
(Mālā) **Necklace**

तारा
(Tārā) **Star**

गाना
(Gānā) **Song**

दादा
(Dādā) **Grandfather**

आया
(Āyā) **Came**

लड़का
(Laṛkā) **Boy**

अपना
(Apnā) **Our**

कमरा
(Kamrā) **Room**

गागर
(Gāgar) **Pot**

सागर
(Sāgar) **Sea**

तालाब
(Tālāb) **Tank**

आकाश
(Ākāsh) **Sky**

पाठ याद कर। चार आम ला। छाता लगाकर चल।
हाथ साफ़ कर। राम लाल माला पहन।

काला बादल आया। अपना कमरा साफ़ कर। जा, बाबा का छाता ला। अहा, चाचा का बाजा बजा। गागर भर कर ला। चाचा ताला लगा गया। टपटप जल बरस पड़ा। दादा गाना गाकर नाच उठा।

(Symbol ि) sounds 'i' as in it

इ की मात्रा इ = ि

द + इ = द + ि = दि

च + इ = च + ि = चि

दिन
(Din) **Day**

लिख
(Likh) **Write**

नित
(Nit) **Everyday**

गिन
(Gin) **Count**

सिर
(Sir) **Head**

पिता
(Pitā) **Father**

शिला
(Shilā) **Rock**

किधर
(Kidhar) **Where**

तिलक
(Tilak) **Boy's name**

निकल
(Nikal) **To come out**

फिसल
(Phisal) **To slip**

किताब
(Kitāb) **Book**

हिसाब
(Hisāb) **Account**

विचार
(Vichār) **Thought**

गिलास
(Gilās) **Tumbler**

चिड़िया
(Chiṛiā) **Sparrow**

टिकिया
(Ṭikiyā) **Tablet**

हरिन
(Harin) **Deer**

बछिया
(Bachhiyā) **Calf**

डलिया
(Ḍaliyā) **Basket**

धनिया
(Dhaniā) **Coriander**

दिन निकल आया । दस तक गिन । अपना पाठ लिख । नित पाठशाला जा । किताब ला, हिसाब कर । विचार कर काम कर । माता पिता का कहना मान । शिला पर गिर जाएगा । गिलास का चित्र बना । चिड़िया मत पकड़ । इस किताब पर अपना नाम लिख ।

(Symbol ी) sounds as 'ī' in keel

ई की मात्रा ई = ि

ग + ई = ग + ी = गी

थ + इ = थ + ी = थी

भीम
(Bhīm) **Boy's name**

बीज
(Bīj) **Seed**

गीत
(Gīt) **Song**

तीर
(Tīr) **Arrow**

नीम
(Nīm) **Name of a tree**

जीभ
(Jībh) **Tongue**

ठीक
(Ṭhīk) **Right**

पगड़ी
(Pagṛī) **Turban**

छतरी
(Chhatrī) **Umbrella**

मीठा
(Mīṭhā) **Sweet**

वीणा
(Vīṇā) **Musical Instrument**

सीता
(Sītā) **Girl's name**

चटनी
(Chaṭnī) **Sauce**

फीता
(Phītā) **Tape**

ककड़ी
(Kakṛī) **Cucumber**

लकड़ी
(Lakṛī) **Wood**

अपनी
(Apanī) **Our**

नानी
(Nānī) **Grandmother**

गाड़ी
(Gāṛī) **Train**

चाची
(Chāchī) **Aunty**

शीशा
(Shīshā) **Mirror**

नीला
(Nīlā) **Blue**

पीला
(Pīlā) **Yellow**

गरीब
(Garīb) **Poor**

हरीश की कमीज़ ला। अपनी पगड़ी साफ़ कर। काली छतरी ला। नीला पीला फीता बना। गरीब की सहायता कर। नानी गाड़ी पर चढ़। चाची चटनी ला। सीता अपनी वीणा बजा। जीभ न निकाल। अहा, ककड़ी बकरी खा गई।

(Symbol ु) sounds as 'u' (as in put)

उ की मात्रा उ = ु

प + उ = प + ु = पु

त + उ = त + ु = तु

पुल
(Pul) **Bridge**

सुन
(Sun) **Listen**

चुप
(Chup) **Silent**

बुध
(Budh) **Wednesday**

कुश
(Kush) **An Indian King**

गुरु
(Guru) **Teacher**

गुलाब
(Gulāb) **Rose**

धनुष
(Dhanush) **Bow**

घुटना
(Ghuṭnā) **Knee**

मथुरा
(Mathurā) **Mathura a city's name**

सुथरा
(Suthrā) **Clean**

कुरता
(Kurtā) **Shirt**

लुहार
(Luhār) **Blacksmith**

दुकान
(Dukān) **Shop**

यमुना
(Yamunā) **Yamuna a river**

बुलबुल
(Bulbul) **Nightingale**

कुटिया
(Kuṭiyā) **Hut**

फुलवाड़ी
(Phulwāṛī) **Nursery**

पुल पर चढ़ । यमुना जा कर नहा आ । गुरु जी की कुटिया पर जा । धनुष बाण चलाना सीख । साफ़ सुथरा कुरता पहन । रुपया उधार न ला । बुधवार लुहार की दुकान खुली थी । वह बुलबुल उड़ गई ।

(Symbol ू) sounds as 'ū' (as in who)

ऊ की मात्रा   ऊ = ू

ज + ऊ = ज + ू = जू   द + ऊ = द + ू = दू

फूल
(Phūl) **Flower**

चूहा
(Chūhā) **Rat**

झूला
(Jhūlā) **Swing**

दूध
(Dūdh) **Milk**

जूता
(Jūtā) **Shoes**

मूली
(Mūlī) **Radish**

धूप
(Dhūp) **Sunrays**

बूढ़ा
(Būṛhā) **An Oldman**

अमरूद
(Amrūd) **Guava**

चूस
(Chūs) **Suck**

भूखा
(Bhūkhā) **Hungry**

खजूर
(Khajūr) **Date**

धूल
(Dhūl) **Dust**

आलू
(Ālū) **Potato**

रूमाल
(Rūmāl) **Handkerchief**

फूल पर धूल न डाल । आम चूस, दूध पी । भूखा न रह । सखी मूली न खा । मीठा अमरूद खा । जूता भीग गया । खजूर पर न चढ़ । रूपरानी झूला झूल । भगवान की पूजा कर । चूहा भाग गया । रामपुर जा, शहतूत ला ।

ऋ की मात्रा ऋ = ृ

क + ऋ = क + ृ = कृ　　　न + ऋ = न + ृ = नृ

मृग (Mrig) **Deer**	ऋण (Riṇ) **Debt**	घृणा (Ghriṇā) **Hate**
तृण (Triṇ) **Grass**	ऋतु (Ritu) **Season**	अमृत (Amrit) **Nectar**
वृक्ष (Vriksh) **Tree**	भृगु (Bhrigu) **An Indian Saint**	हृदय (Hridaya) **Heart**
गृह (Grih) **House**	कृपा (Kripā) **Please**	पृथ्वी (Prithvī) **Earth**
घृत (Ghrit) **Ghee**	वृथा (Vrithā) **Story**	

मृग तृण चर रहा है। दीन पर कृपा कर। माता-पिता का ऋण चुका। अमृत लाल, गर्मी की ऋतु आई। बहुत घृत न खा। पृथ्वीराज हार गया। भृगु ऋषि था।

(Symbol `) e

ए की मात्रा ए = `

ज + ए = ज + ` = जे          स + ए = स + ` = से

बेर (Ber) **Berry**	नेता (Netā) **Leader**	केशव (Keshav) **A Boy's name**
शेर (Sher) **Tiger**	चेला (Chelā) **Disciple**	अकेला (Akelā) **Alone**
सेब (Seb) **Apple**	बेटा (Beṭā) **Son**	देखना (Dekhnā) **To see**
खेत (Khet) **Field**	ठेला (Ṭhelā) **Cart**	भेजना (Bhejnā) **To send**
पेड़ (Peṛ) **Tree**	मेंढक (Mẽḍhak) **Frog**	अजमेर (Ajmer) **A City's name**

बेर का पेड़ देख। एक मीठा सेब ला। गुरु जी की सेवा कर। नेता जी की जय। जूठी जलेबी न खा। चेला चमेली का फूल लाया। केशव लेट कर न पढ़। बेटा सुरेश, केला अकेला न खा। ठेला पटरी पर रुक गया। अजमेर से रेल आई।

(Symbol ै) sounds as 'ai' (as in Maina)

ऐ की मात्रा ऐ = ै

क + ऐ = क + ै = कै   ह + ऐ = ह + ै = है

बैल
(Bail) **Bullock**

पैर
(Pair) **Foot**

सैर
(Sair) **Walk**

वैर
(Vair) **Enmity**

बैठ
(Baiṭh) **To sit**

पैसा
(Paisā) **Coin**

थैला
(Thailā) **Bag**

मैना
(Mainā) **Name of a bird**

मैला
(Mailā) **Dirty**

भैया
(Bhaiyā) **Brother**

तैराक
(Tairāk) **Swimmer**

मैदान
(Maidān) **Ground**

वैशाख
(Vaishākh) **Name of an Indian month**

कैलाश
(Kailāsh) **A Boy's name**

फैलना
(Phailnā) **To spread**

राम शाम सवेरे सैर किया कर। मेरा पैसा दे। तैराक हाथ पैर मारता है। थैला मैला न कर। चैन से बैठ। बैल हल चलाता है। जैसा काम वैसा दाम। यह फुटबाल का मैदान है। यह बैठक कैलाश की है। आज वैशाख का पहला दिन है।

(Symbol ो) sounds as 'o' (as in Pole)

ओ की मात्रा ओ = ो

ग + ओ = ग + ो = गो

द + ओ = द + ो = दो

मोर
(Mor) **Peacock**

शोर
(Shor) **Noise**

बोल
(Bol) **To speak**

गोल
(Gol) **Round**

कोट
(Koṭ) **Coat**

टोपी
(Ṭopī) **Cap**

धोबी
(Dhobī) **Washerman**

रोटी
(Roṭī) **Bread**

छोटी
(Chhoṭī) **Small**

होली
(Holī) **An Indian festival**

तोता
(Tota) **Parrot**

झोला
(Jholā) **Bag**

घोड़ा
(Ghoṛā) **Horse**

कोयल
(Koyal) **Cuckoo**

सोमवार
(Somwār) **Monday**

मोर नाच रहा है। मेरा कोट ला दो। सब से मीठा बोल। टोकरा न तोड़ो। पृथ्वी गोल है। धोबी धोती धोकर लाया। सोहन घोड़ा लाया। सब पर दया करना सीखो। धीरे–धीरे चलो। शोर न मचाओ। सोमवार होली है।

(Symbol ौ) sounds as 'au' or 'ow' (as in Owl)

औ की मात्रा औ = ौ

क + औ = क + ौ = कौ　　**च + औ = च + ौ = चौ**

फौज
(Fauj) **Army**

लौट
(Lauṭ) **To come back**

दौड़
(Dauṛ) **To run**

कौन
(Kaun) **Who**

औरत
(Aurat) **Woman**

चौधरी
(Chaudharī) **Leader**

नौका
(Naukā) **Boat**

कौआ
(Kauā) **Crow**

पौधा
(Paudhā) **Plant**

चौथा
(Chauthā) **Fourth**

मौसम
(Mausam) **Weather**

गौतम देव
(Gautam Dev) **A boy's name**

दौलत
(Daulat) **Money**

लोमड़ी
(Lomṛī) **Fox**

सौदागर
(Saudāgar) **Merchant**

चौकीदार
(Chaukīdār) **Watchman**

खिलौना
(Khilaunā) **Toy**

फ़ौज किला जीत कर लौट आई। दौड़ कर गौ को पकड़ो। औरत से मखौल मत करो। कौन पौधा तोड़ता है ? कौआ नौका पर बैठा है। रमेश शाम का चौथा भाई है। दौलत राम को चौधरी बना दो। नौकर बोझ उठा रहा है। सौदागर चौकीदार को धमकाता है। यह खिलौना गौतम देव का है।

(Symbol ं) sounds as 'n' (as in Pink)

अं की मात्रा अं = ं

द + अं = द + ं = दं　　　　र + अं = र + ं = रं

रंग
(Rang) **Colour**

ठंडा
(Ṭhanḍā) **Cold**

बसंत
(Basant) **Spring season**

पतंग
(Patang) **Kite**

अंगूर
(Angūr) **Grapes**

हिंदी
(Hindī) **Hindi**

हिंसक
(Hinsak) **Fierce**

सिंह
(Singh) **Lion**

कंघा
(Kanghā) **Comb**

सुंदर
(Sundar) **Beautiful**

संगति
(Sangati) **Society**

अंगिया
(Angiyā) **Bodice**

संखिया
(Sãkhiyā) **Arsenic**

भौंकना
(Bhãuknā) **To bark**

खींचना
(khĩchnā) **To pull**

मुझे लाल रंग अच्छा लगता है। शाम बसंत के दिन पतंग उड़ाता है। मीठे अंगूर अमृत फल है। हिंदी भारत की राजभाषा है। मोर कैसा सुंदर लगता है। सिंह हिंसक पशु है। यह अंगिया मलमल की है। शीला की संखिया खाने से मृत्यु हो गई। बुरों की संगति से बचो। कुत्ता टांग खींच कर भौंकता है।

चन्द्र बिन्दु तथा अः की मात्रा अँ = ँ, अः = ः

ह + अँ = ह + ँ = हँ

द + अः = द + ः = दः

मुँह
(Mũh) **Mouth**

ऊँट
(Ū̃ṭ) **Camel**

गाँव
(Gā̃v) **Village**

दाँत
(Dā̃t) **Teeth**

आँख
(Ā̃kh) **Eye**

टाँग
(Ṭā̃g) **Leg**

छः
(Chhah) **Six**

पुनः
(Punah) **Again**

दुःख
(Dukh) **Trouble**

बंदर के मुँह पर लाली होती है। ऊँट बहुत ऊँचा जानवर है, उसकी चार बड़ी-बड़ी टाँगें होती हैं। राम जब गाँव जाता है तब ऊँट पर चढ़ता है। दूध की भाँति दाँत साफ़ कर। प्रातः उठकर आँख साफ़ कर। छः लिटर दूध ला। राम दीन के दुःख पर न हँस। देखना शाम, पुनः झूठ न बोलना।

बेला रानी, बेला रानी।

बेला रानी, बड़ी सयानी॥

तख्ती पर लिखती थी बेला।

बन्दर आया लेकर केला॥

बन्दर बोला — तख्ती दोगी ?

बदले में यह केला लोगी ?

डर कर भागी बेला रानी।

मर गई बेला जी की नानी॥

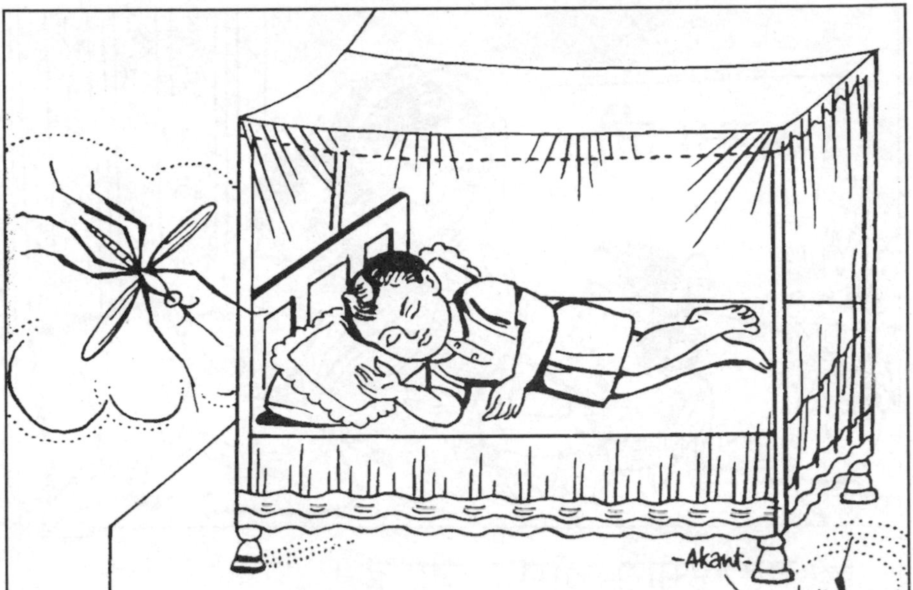

मच्छर सदा रात को आता।
काट-काट मच्छर भाग जाता॥
मच्छरदानी आज मँगाओ।
अंदर लेटो मौज उड़ाओ॥
मच्छरदानी है मंगवाई।
मच्छर की अब आफत आई॥
देखो, अन्दर बच्चा सोता।
बाहर भन-भन मच्छर रोता॥

यह हमारी अम्मा जी हैं।

हम बच्चे अम्मा को बहुत प्यार करते हैं।

अम्मा हमें लड्डू खिलाती है।

अम्मा हमें खीर खिलाती है।

अम्मा मुन्ने को खिलाती है।

अम्मा के बिना हमें कुछ अच्छा नहीं लगता।

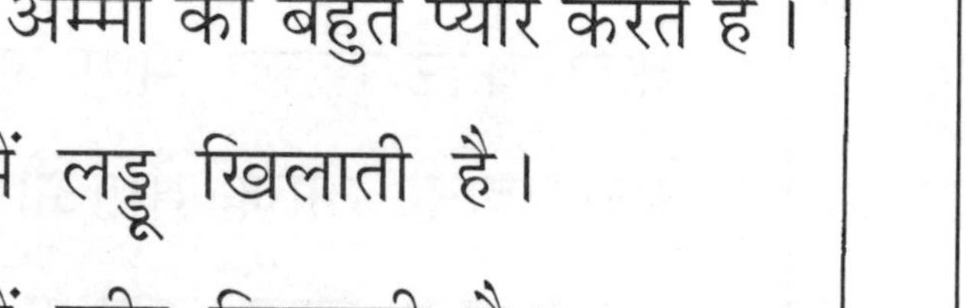

Hindi	Hindi in Roman Script	Meaning
पर	Par	On
चढ़	Charh	Get on
भर	Bhar	Fill
उठ	Uṭh	Get up/Stand
अब	Ab	Now
चल	Chal	Go
बच कर	Bach kar	Carefully/Safely
कर	Kar	Do
बर्तन	Bartan	Vessel
रख	Rakh	Put
न बन	Na ban	Do not become
ला	Lā	Bring
लगाकर	Lagā kar	Having put on
राम लाल	Rām Lāl	Name of a male person
पहन	Pahan	Put on/Wear
बादल	Bādal	Cloud
आया	Āyā	Came
अपना	Apnā	His/Your/Her/My
जा	Jā	Go
बाबा	Bābā	Grandfather/Old man
अहा	Ahā	Laugh
का	Kā	Of

Hindi	Hindi in Roman Script	Meaning
बाजा	Bājā	Musical Instrument
बजा	Bajā	To play
ताला	Tālā	Lock
लगा गया	Lagā gayā	Fixed
टप टप	Ṭap ṭap	Dripping
बरस पड़ा	Baras paṛā	Rained
गाकर	Gā kar	Having sung
नाच उठा	Nāch uṭhā	Started dancing
निकल आया	Nīkal āyā	Dawned
दस	Das	Ten
तक	Tak	Upto
पाठशाला	Pāṭhshālā	School
काम	Kām	Work
माता	Mātā	Mother
कहना मान	Kahnā mān	Obey
गिर जाएगा	Gir jāegā	Will fall
चित्र	Chittra	Picture
बना	Banā	Make/draw
मत	Mat	Do not
पकड़	Pakaṛ	Catch/hold
इस	Is	This
नाम	Nām	Name

Hindi	Hindi in Roman Script	Meaning
चढ़	Charh	Climb/ Go up
नहा आ	Nahā ā	Have a bath
जी	Jī	Used for respect
कुटिआ	Kuṭiā	Cottage
बाण	Bāṇ	Arrow
चलाना	Chalānā	Shoot/ Drive
सीख	Sīkh	Learn
रुपया	Rupayā	Rupee (Indian money)
उधार	Udhār	Borrow
न	Nā	Not
खुली	Khulī	Open
थी	Thī	Was
उड़ गई	Uṛ gaī	Flew away
डाल	Ḍāl	Put
पी	Pī	Drink
रह	Rah	Stay
सखी	Sakhī	Friend
मीठा	Mīṭhā	Sweet
भीग	Bhīg	To get wet
रूपरानी	Rūp Rānī	Name of a girl
भगवान	Bhagwān	God
पूजा	Pūjā	Worship

Hindi	Hindi in Roman Script	Meaning
भाग गया	Bhāg gayā	Ran away
रामपुर	Rāmpur	Name of a city
शहतूत	Shahtūt	Mulberry
चर रहा है	Char rahā hai	Is grazing
दीन	Dīn	Name of a male person
कृपा	Kripā	Kindness
चुका	Chukā	To pay back
अमृत लाल	Amrit Lāl	Name of a male person
गर्मी	Garmī	Heat/summer
बहुत	Bahut	A lot
पृथ्वी राज	Prithvī Rāj	Name of a male person
हार गया	Hār gayā	Was lost
देख	Dekh	Look
एक	Ek	One
गुरु	Guru	Teacher
सेवा	Sewā	Service
जय	Jay	Victory
जूठी	Jūṭhī	Left over
जलेबी	Jalebī	An Indian sweet
चेला	Chelā	Disciple
चमेली	Chamelī	Jasmine
लाया	Lāyā	Brought

Hindi	Hindi in Roman Script	Meaning
केशव	Keshav	Name of a male person
लेट	Laṭe	To die down
सुरेश	Suresh	Name of a male person or female person
केला	Kelā	Banana
अकेला	Akelā	Alone
पटरी	Paṭarī	Rail track
रुक गया	Ruk gayā	Stopped
रेल	Rel	Train
अजमेर	Ajmer	Name of a city in India
शाम	Shām	In the evening
सवेरा	Saverā	In the morning
मेरा	Merā	My
दे	De	Give
मारता है	Mārtā hai	Moves
चैन से	Chain se	Quietly
हल	Hal	Plough
चलाता है	Chalātā hai	Draws
जैसा	Jaisā	Such
काम	Kām	Work
वैसा	Vaisā	Exactly/Such
दाम	Dām	Wages

Hindi	Hindi in Roman Script	Meaning
बैठक	Baiṭhak	Sitting room
आज	Āj	Today
वैशाख	Vaishākh	Name of an Indian month
नाच रहा है	Nāch rahā hai	Is dancing
सब से	Sab se	With all
टोकरा	Ṭokrā	Basket
तोड़ो	Toṛo	Brake
पृथ्वी	Prithvī	Earth
धोती	Dhotī	Indian dress
धोकर	Dho kar	Having washed
मोहन	Mohan	Name of a male person
सब	Sabh	All
दया करना	Dayā karnā	To be kind
सीखो	Sīkho	Learn
धीरे धीरे	Dhīre dhīre	Slowly
मचाओ	Machāo	Make
किला	Kilā	Fort
जीत कर	Jīt kar	Having conquered
गौ	Gau	Cow
पकड़ो	Pakṛo	Catch
मखौल	Makhaul	Joke

Hindi	Hindi in Roman Script	Meaning
मत करो	Mat karo	Do not make/do
रमेश	Ramesh	Name of a male person
शाम	Shām	Name of a male person
चौधरी	Chaudharī	Chief
नौकर	Naukar	Servant
बोझ	Bojh	Weight
धमकाता	Dhamkātā	Frightens
खिलौना	Khilaunā	Toy
गौतम देव	Gautam Dev	Name of a male person
उठा रहा है	Uṭhā rahā hai	Is lifting
मुझे	Mujhe	To me
उड़ाता है	Uṛātā hai	Flies
अमृत	Amrit	Very sweet
भारत	Bhārat	Other name for India
राज भाषा	Rāj bhāshā	Official language
लाल	Lāl	Red
कैसा	Kaisā	How
पशु	Pashū	Animal
लगता है	Lagtā hai	Looks
मलमल	Malmal	Muslin
शीला	Shīlā	Name of a female person
मृत्यु	Mrityū	Death

Hindi	Hindi in Roman Script	Meaning
बुरों	Buron	Bad people
बचो	Bacho	Keep away
कुत्ता	Kuttā	Dog
टांग	Ṭāng	Leg
खींच कर	Khīnch kar	Having pulled
लाली	Lālī	Redness
बंदर	Bandar	Monkey
बहुत	Bohut	A lot
ऊँचा	Ū̃chā	Tall/high
जानवर	Jānvar	Animal
उसकी	Uskī	Its/His/Her
बड़ी बड़ी	Baṛī baṛī	Big
होती हैं	Hoti haĩ	Are
जब	Jab	When
जाता है	Jātā hai	Goes
तब	Tab	Then
चढ़ता	Chaṛhtā	Rides
दूध	Dūdh	Milk
भाँति	Bhāntī	Like
प्रातः	Prātah	In the morning
लिटर	Liṭar	Litre
राम दीन	Rām Dīn	Name of a male person

Hindi	Hindi in Roman Script	Meaning
हँस	Hãs	Laugh
देखना	Dekhnā	Having seen/look/see
झूठ	Jhūṭh	Lie
बोलना	Bolnā	Speak
बेला रानी	Bela Rānī	Name of a female person
स्यानी	Syānī	Wise
तख्ती	Takhtī	Piece of wood used for writing in India
लिखती	Likhtī	Writes
आया	Āyā	Came
लेकर	Lekar	Having brought
बोला	Bolā	Spoke
दोगी	Dogī	Will give
बदले	Badle	Exchange
में	Mẽ	In
यह	Yah	This
लोगी	Logī	Will take
डर	Ḍar	Frightened/fear
भागी	Bhāgī	Ran
मर गई	Mar gaī	Died
नानी	Nānī	Grandmother/ Mother's mother

Hindi	Hindi in Roman Script	Meaning
मच्छर	Machhar	Mosquito
सदा	Sadā	Always
रात को	Rāt ko	At nights
आता	Ātā	Comes
काट	Kāṭ	To cut
भाग जाता	Bhāg jātā	Runs
मच्छरदानी	Machhardānī	Mosquito net
आज	Āj	Today
हमारी	Hamārī	Our
जी	Jī	Word used for respect
बच्चे	Bacche	Children
प्यार	Piār	Love
लड्डू	Laḍḍū	Indian sweet
खिलाती	Khilātī	Gives to eat
खीर	Khīr	Indian sweet dish
मुन्ना	Munnā	Child
बिना	Binā	Without
अच्छा	Achhā	Good